INSPIRED BY K

Inspired By K

An Inspirational Chapbook

KENSHAE WESTMORELAND

Eleven11 Publishing

Contents

1
INTRODUCTION

1	Keep Pushing	4
2	Super Woman	10
Notes		16
3	Skin Vs Reality	17
4	Movement	21
5	The Sun Will Shine	26
Notes		29

vi ~ Contents

6	Act Now	30
7	Letter to Heaven	34
8	Fighter	40

Notes 44

9	Growing Up	45
10	Only be Me	52
11	Do Not Give Up	56

12
QUESTIONS FOR YOU

GOALS

GOALS

1

Introduction

Hello, Are you tired of being mad? Do you need advice on how to handle tough situations? Are you going through a hard time and need some encouragement? The universe will place obstacles in your life so that you will become wiser. You are in full control of the life you create for yourself. No matter what you go through never give up on your goals. My goal is to put some life situations in perspective so that you can understand the different views and outcomes. You can control everything and everybody around you.

If you are like me sometimes books get

long and boring, but this book is written in poem format. Every poem is designed to give off positive vibrations into your life. It will be clear and understandable to read for all ages. One has studied for three years to be able to give off positive vibrations readings with the help of some of the top influencers in the world. In the future, this book will help you think wiser about making your decisions and enlighten readers from their bad decisions. I would like to be the first to tell you that a mistake is only a weak decision that you made. Every day you wake up you have to make decisions. The life you create is from your decisions made.

Over the year's I have mastered the good and the bad days they so-called say we have. Every day can be a good day unless you have not taken the right steps in good everyday living. You will feel unbalanced when you are not practicing daily deeds. The secret to having good days are doing good things. Practicing good deeds include doing something nice or doing something right whether than wrong. Even the small things you don't pay attention to matter the most. You have to train your mind to act as a great person daily so it will become second nature. I have put together this book of poems to give you a fun engaging read. There will also be a note and goal section so that you can write down your goals and any notes as needed.

Chapter 1

Keep Pushing

Stuck in between ready but not right now,

You will be stuck do it now.

Small goals to big goals still are proud,

Never let anyone put you down.

This your pass to the abundance,

and I can tell you how,

I'm here to tell you all your tribulations are to be faced with a smile.

No more frowning.

No more crying.

No more throwing in the towel.

Been there and done that,

and it's been a while.
Thank the universe for guidance for one doesn't know-how.

Now ask yourself where were you then?

And look at you now.

You wouldn't think you made it through but it's the power of a smile.

Always stay positive and make yourself proud,

For you control your actions with or without a crowd.

Be careful who you let around,

Energies are real and they get wild.

When you protect your peace there's no need to get loud,

The sun will shine so bright you won't notice a cloud.

Keep the positive thinking way more than mild,

You will achieve everything that you dreamed of as a child.

The time is now and will forever be,

Try laughing in a bad situation and you will see.

It is the turnaround of the problem for me,

and one knows it may be hard but Ima gives you the tea.

All you got to do is believe it's okay and the universe will receive.

Now that the universe has received,

it is time to do your deeds.

Get on the good chart and get all your needs,

Achieve your goals, and plant all your seeds.

Every problem is a distraction to test your breed,

Never fall under pressure that's how you succeed.

If it's yours then it's yours forever it will be,

It is the distractions that make you lose the vision you see.

Never give up and it won't be easy.

Compete with the old you every season,

You make decisions for a reason.

Every outcome may not be good but you are still breathing,

Be grateful for living and complain about nothing.

This one way to turn nothing into something.

Affirmation

" One will choose my decisions wisely for one will live with the decision made. One will learn from their mistakes. I will become a wiser decision-maker so that my life will flourish. "

Chapter 2

Super Woman

"Women are powerful, women are bold, women are the most important people."

We bring life,

We bring happiness,

and We bring love.

W for wiser,

O for outgoing,

M for Mature,

E for excellent,

and N for nice empowered human beings.

Women hold lives,

that's how we are existing.

A woman is the purest form of perfection.

Who runs the world?

Girls, known that since back then.

And, salute to Rosa Parks for taking that stand.

"For I'm a woman, stronger than I ever been."

Remind yourself queen, cuz it comes from within.

If it wasn't for us it would be no men.

Women are beautiful that's how it's always been.

I remember I use to write in cursive beautiful, beautifully.

Some things never change,

a woman is a beast.

At peace with herself was her biggest enemy,

And having confidence brought all them angels free.

Some fighting from depression,

because happiness is what they see.

So, when you see peace is where one wants to be.

Keep a smile on your face,

cuz he will set you free.

They don't know where one comes from,

They just know what they see.

Women are so bold!

Count her in and she won't fold.

Hardworking women worth way more than gold.

Inspired by the women,

who couldn't make it to see old?

And women who fight for their goal.

Prayers up to the "missing" who haven't made it home.

I promise you that these women are really strong.

It's women who can't see or talk to their kids on the phone.

I have seen my granny in a coma,

now she blows up my phone.

So grateful she's here I don't care if she can't walk.

From a trait, and two strokes she was fighting for it all.

And I can call her today to remind her that she is strong.

A woman's heart is just like a baby soul.

Walk up, and men open the door.

Queen wakes up and takes advantage of more.

"She strong, bold, and gifted."

Been hurt a couple of times but she still lifted.

Women rule the world and I'm not going against it.

That small rock is a diamond already existing.

A diamond in the ruff hey?

Ya, you feel what I'm saying.

Cuz you know you love your boo,

she always slaying.

It's a woman thing,

it's never changing.

Notes

Take notes as you read!

Chapter 3

Skin Vs Reality

" The skin should never determine the respect you give one another. The skin should be a feature that a human being has. We all are different for the bones to start the same."

Pushed around, pushed away nobody wanted me to stay.

I am a female,

no, you a slave they say,

I have no rights segregation took them away.

My mind so gone, can't stand for my respect,

so what ima do now in the color of black.

Under my skin, it's bones like the white man,

so how are we different because they gave us a title and nobody could fix it.

What about the 13th amendment?

Says, " slavery and involuntary servitude except as a punishment for a crime."

So basically you a slave at any given time.

Working for a little money, and accused of crimes.

First, it was slaves, now it's criminals.

Why we get so many titles it's unbelievable?

I am a female under my skin,

Harriet Tubman freed the slaves,

that was a black woman.

Black Panther's leader got shot,

they don't ever want to see a black man on the spot.

Rapist, killer, robber, titles again!

Why he get shot without a gun in his hand?

Mr. King got shot just for having a dream.

We will get no respect just because of the skin that we are in.

Racism starts with you,

One will take a stand.

Can we hold each other hands,

Forget about the titles and be a better friend.

Do what is right to make America great again.

Chapter 4

Movement

"Inspired by the movement, is inspired by K, which is inspired by me, and one thinks movement steady change."

Where I'm from it's like the jungle and I'm the prey,

Like back in the day when Harriet Tubman freed the slaves.

Inspired by the movement.

I wake folks up every day.

Got a dream like Martin, just in a different way,

but the same how slaves sing is the same as how rappers slang.

One thinks we are living in a modern way.

So, pray, stack, and pray.

Cuz trouble doesn't last always.

Movement this, the movement that,

don't let it fade away.

You surrounded by the movement,

Shit, still the same.

So, thank whom you worship,

for we live a better way.

Don't get it twisted the hood is where one stayed.

Where you heard gunshots throughout the day.

Is it a police officer or a snake,

who's to say?

Like back then,

the streets never safe.

Inspired by the hustlers making away.

Inspired by the movement.

I'm inspired by the movement.

Not like running fast,

but the thing the president abusing.

The alternative way get us in trouble but people are tired of losing.

You got to have money, or you are snoozing.

This world will make you feel like you losing,

Although, people give up,

not me I'm cruising.

Harriet Tubman could do it.

MLK did,

Hussle took the role to lead on a good stand.

Then it's me,

a savior girl at hand.

One has been feeling this,

been doing the plan.

Everybody can be strong, Just take the lead's hand.

Lead you in the direction for all you do is win.

Inspired by the movement.

Inspired by K.

You not hearing me,

I wake people up every day.

Inspired to inspire is a successful wave.

Get inspired,

B.C time our ancestors were living in caves.

Never get distracted by the movement for I'm saved.

Chapter 5

The Sun Will Shine

Feeling bad luck or do you feel like nothing going your way?

Everything just going down the drain,

So bad you can't even get a place to stay.

Maybe money running low and you ready to give up any day.

You not on your own don't go out that way,

People go through things every day.

Relax, breath, and pray,

Sunshine is on its way,

Don't give up not today.

Even when it gets hard,

It is a happy lane,

Take your happiness seriously because it's hard to maintain.

Stay positive so you can have a better day than yesterday.

Grow and heal that long-life pain,

Keep pushing through change gone come,

blessings will gone rain.

Today the day you change the thinking of the brain,

You will always grow and nothing remain the same.

Keep your faith in the name of his vein,

You beat the last test blessings is what you should claim.

When something goes wrong think of the next thing,

Manifest your dreams, stay in your lane.

The sun will shine after the rain,

Never focus on the pain. Tackle your goals to maintain,

Happiness is key.

Happiness shall keep you in your lane.

Happiness is so strong you will forget the pain.

Notes

Notes for you!

Chapter 6

Act Now

It's time that you get up and act now,

It's time for you to make everyone say wow.

Do it because it makes you proud,

Don't worry about how.

For if you thought it then it's in the works right now,

Everything you think you were going to do has already been down.

It is the decisions you make that will give you your how,

Whatever it is make sure it's your commitment,

Anytime you see yourself,

you see yourself winning.

Give yourself a reason to keep pushing through the seasons.

You won't have to worry about what if,

Actions are not for the weakening

Be prepared to work hard,

Write everything down.

Keep your vision clear so you can feel it near,

Act now not later for the door is right there.

When you feel bubbly about your achievements,

You are moving in the right direction.

When you moving toward your purpose,

There is no need to stress perfection.

When you doing what is right, there will be no rejection.

The world is yours,

You will feel no more neglect.

If you feeling scared then it's time NOW!

Affirmation

" One will act now because there are no promises for tomorrow. One knows it is time when I feel scared. I will not ignore or confuse the feeling. If I am scared, I am ready."

Chapter 7

Letter to Heaven

I miss you, granny, that's that

Matter of fact I wanna tell you,

I want cha back.

Also, reflect on the past and laugh,

I know you a Lil older,

so I won't go fast.

I'm highly upset that I made it last to see your cold body on the scratch bed,

All I can remember I was holding your hand.

And I'll never ask why,

because it was always the plan,

Everybody time has gone come,

just don't know when.

Just let the letter begin,

I need a friend,

I can't pretend,

but I'm telling you I'm stronger than I ever been.

Lost everything but didn't bend,

Never stress about anything because with god I'm gone win.

Thank you for showing me how to love man,

And keeping my peace through the strong wind.

I'm not sad because I see what you were going through,

I'm not sad because family is all you were holding on to.

I'm not sad because god got his hands on you,

And forever will I cherish the moments I have with you.

Thank you for teaching me how to push through,

I am chosen and I had no clue.

Realized the world was mine when I lost you,

The family broke up you were the glue.

It's like you got sicker out the blue,

But the process was right in our review.

In reality, if we paid attention to you and your every move,

From the last time playing Uno with you and you were up and moving smooth,

We cooked and cleaned,

you were always on my team,

But in the process, it was all just the end.

No one never knew but I read,
and I understand,

I felt your relief through your hand.

I made you laugh before the last stage,

I was there with you through your last days.

Trying my best to save you in the toughest way,

Just remember you would call,

and call folks but I was a call away.

We click tight like chains that won't break,

Together laughter is the sound we make.

Oh, I how I miss you, granny.

Affirmation

" I will not get angry at my creator for taking what is his. I understand our loved ones are given to us temporarily. I will remember the good memories and never ask the question of why. I will ask for strength and prosperity."

Chapter 8

Fighter

Be a fighter.

Beat every obstacle you run into life.

Big or small you will win using all your might,

Set that goal up,

and tackle the goals every night.

There will be mountains and bears,

But don't ever lose sight.

There is no weapon form against you so you never lose a fight,

Whatever done in the dark will come to the light.

Stop using your energy if it's not for something right,

Fight!

Achieve all your goals and fly high as a kite,

Some fighting from depression waking up throughout the night.

Most fighting for a wage because their skin not white,

Be a fighter.

While everyone else is being a doubter, One decided to be the believer.

Believe anything that occurs in my life is for a reason,

Stay positive that's is how to get to the next season.

No rain, sleet, nor snow is gone stop you from rising,

it's kind of like surviving.

After practicing for so long having to fight through,

You realize every problem was meant to build you.

Affirmation

"I will not back down from any fight. I am a winner; I will win every obstacle that comes my way. Obstacles are there to make you go harder. The only way to defeat obstacles is with a smile."

Notes

Take notes as you read!

Chapter 9

Growing Up

Wait I don't know what to say.

Wait I don't how to say it,

wait... wait...

When I was 12 years old, only twelve,

I was offered to have sex for money with some men but told not to snitch.

That's when it all began.

I had a shape more like 18 but I was a baby who knew nothing about brutality.

Went to school shook out my skin,

about this man who once told me to bend.

I couldn't stop thinking I couldn't stop shaking,

a panic attack was awakening.

I had to tell and there was no thinking about it.

I had therapy and he got in trouble,

but that wasn't the end it began another struggle.

At 17 we had to move because they were selling the property.

We had a month then a week and my mom didn't have that kind of money!

Next thing you know on the streets we were all struggling from house to house.

I knew this couldn't be true.

A high school junior at Maplewood and my grades were slacking too.

I had a wreck,

the hood flew up while I was driving to save who?

My mom got into a fight with her brother,

Had to leave that house she didn't know what else to do.

She had to stay strong for us too,

It was a struggle but we made it through.

I turned 18 and it all was the same DECA in school was the only thing that keeps me sane.

Before the DECA trip,

my granny had surgery on her brain.

To be specific,

an aneurysm that would have taken her away.

She missed me walk across the stage.

She missed the accomplishments I made.

She was still in rehab trying to recover from her brain.

Her whole left side went blank.

But wait it ain't over let me tell you about this struggle.

August was here. It was the beginning of my biggest fear!

Grandad passed and my granny passed 5 days from him.

They were great,

my granny was in rehab couldn't move to even see them.

August 23rd through the 28th was heartbreaking to hear.

I had to start the class was my biggest fear,

Granny didn't know her husband had passed although he was near.

She felt it and was ready to go with him it was clear.

Crying and praying by her side.

I would have never thought it was coming in a blink of an eye.

I understood she was ready and tired.

I almost gave up,

all I could do was cry.

I can't ask God why?

Don't do it please granny try.

She had been through a lot and you could tell she was tired.

Laying in the hospice bed peacefully ready to die.

I had to realize that it was her time.

Lord thank you for my strength because without you she wouldn't be mine.

I'm trying to hold on.

Staying strong for I know I will be fine.

Lord forgive me for my sins before my time.

Chapter 10

Only be Me

If the world ended today,

You can only be you.

Leading and winning is the only thing I see.

Living from place to place how fun that had to be,

Kept a smile on my face,

cuz my creator will set me free.

Here a secret succeeds,

Keep your hopes high and believe what you want to see.

They don't know where one comes from,

They just know what they see.

No matter what one goes through,

No matter how hard it may seem.

Stay positive and be the best you can be,

That's is the key to be free.

I can only be me.

Think about it as wearing a shoe.

The same thing you walk through,

One might not relate to it.

When it's said and done every life belongs to who?

You.

One has no said so for one sees it a different view,

Who are they to tell you what to do?

No explanation needed you were born without a crew,

Do whatever makes you happy too.

Your path and dreams were made for you,

Detox your body so that you can feel new.

Leaving my legacy behind for people to view,

Embracing all the struggles,

and using it as a stepping stool.

I can only me with my flaws too,

Accepting everything even if it's not cool.

Affirmation

" I am enough. I am valued. I am loved. I will accept my flaws and use them as apart of my gift. I am who I am supposed to be." I am me!

Chapter 11

Do Not Give Up

Have you woke up feeling good and all the stoplights were green?

Ain't stunning nobody who was tryna be mean.

Everything works in your favor I mean,

Nothing could make you switch your behavior.

Bills paid now you praising your savior,

And all of a sudden there goes, hater.

Then boom, You get a flat tire!

Now you hanging upside down on the wire,

It's not the end,

You about to go higher.

Don't give up,

It's a test to make you go harder.

Handle the situation with a smile,

Make you're thinking a Lil smarter.

Keep the positive vibes flowing,

Watch the room get brighter,

and solutions to come quicker.

Trails will seem without tribulations.

When you believe everything gone work out for something bigger.

Even when it's your last be a giver,

Do everything with a good leader.

Just don't give up it will make you weaker,

You came this far you a winner.

Quotes

" The moment you were about to give up is the moment you were close to your gift which you were called to act on."

" If you give up now, you lose your chance to win tomorrow."
" Remain focus, to stay focus"

12

Questions For You

1. What do I want In My Life?

2. What am I grateful for?

3. What is missing in life?

4. Do I see the next day as a do-over?

5. Do I listen to what others say about me?

6. Do I have fun?

7. How can I bring more joy into my life?

8. Are you missing opportunities due to pride?

9. Is happiness important to Me?

10. What do I want more of in my life?

Goals

Write down your goals!

Goals

Write down your goals!

www.ingramcontent.com/pod-product-compliance
Lightning Source LLC
Chambersburg PA
CBHW021959290426
44108CB00012B/1142